Dreaming in Color

Ruth Lepson

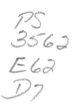

Library of Congress Catalogue card number 79-54882
ISBN 0-914086-27-8

Printed in the United States of America

Cover by Lucy Clark
Design by Carl Kay and Andrea Golden
Photo by Elsa Dorfman
Typeset by Jeffrey Schwartz
Paste-up by Ronna Johnson

With thanks to the following periodicals, in which some of these poems first appeared: *Boston After Dark, Contact II, Maio, Ploughshares, Poet Lore, Squeezebox, The Boston Phoenix, The Chronicle-Telegram, The Real Paper, What She Wants, Women Poems*

The epigraph on page 44, by Fernando Pessoa, is from a poem translated by Jonathan Griffin, published in a collection of Pessoa's work by Carcanet Press Ltd., Oxford, England, 1971.

The publication of this book was assisted by a grant from the Massachusetts Council on the Arts & Humanities.

Alice James Books are published by Alice James Poetry Cooperative, Inc.

ALICE JAMES BOOKS
138 Mt. Auburn Street
Cambridge, Massachusetts 02138

DREAMING IN COLOR

For Bobby,
For my parents and grandparents,
For my friends, and especially Claudia

Contents

LANDSCAPES

HIEROGLYPHS

Living with People

LIVING WITH PEOPLE

Talking is something.
And tables, talking at tables.
Eating and paintings and what walls.
What are they asking.
What am I looking at.
A person talking and eating.
I'm looking at the eyes
that don't look at me.
The foot tapping,
the hungry person,
what is being eaten.

JULY MORNING

Stuck under the pillow, my hand sleeps.
Uncovered, it blushes, pink next to the dark blue sheet.
Held up, it's a white hand filled with lines.
Edges of the mirror become prisms
that catch and multiply last night's purple dress.
Sunlight moves into the room like a feeling—
Is it yellow or is it white?
All the room tilts like a wheel of color.
The next time I wake up I will be married.

FEBRUARY NIGHT

The snowflakes hurl themselves down in chunks to the middle
    of the street.
Things tilt.
I'm a little afraid of an avalanche from the sky.
Chills immobilize my body.
At a quarter to seven, on goes the light of the church steeple.
Tonight you're talking business,
church music from another country.
When the snowflakes are this big they spread out space.

On the day your mother dies,
if it's snowing,
and the cars are stuck,
let's walk down the middle of the street together.
After a few blocks we can wrap our arms
around each other's shoulders
and go walking away,
like two old men in a children's book,
stepping cautiously down the frozen river.

SUCCESS

I. When you're dark
    you come to me.
    In your dark
    two slivers are
    work and family.

    They're deep but they
    narrow. When
    you say you are so
    busy, it
    frightens me, in an
    opaque day,
    clouded with memory.

II. An old dog dreams
    on the rug, his stiff
    legs
    now move like a swan's,
    underwater, loose, and free.

    Your legs
    twitch
    under the blanket.
    All the day they move
    stiffly to push ahead.
    I run,
    but only to catch up.
    They run, to be loved.
    They have a memory.

14

ANOTHER SUNSET

for M.L.

No men, no bridges
can be found
under this salt water
rushing over my knees.
You read on the beach
about medicine and art;
you sweat all over the magazine;
you cover your eyes˙
with it: there is pressure
over the bridge of your nose.
Meanwhile, I am drowning.
You have no notion,
and, after I drown,
I walk back and don't say
too much about it.
Are you my ankles.
I am your bread:
I have soaked in too much salt.
You have nothing to ask me for,
and we drive home,
colored by another sunset.

MELODRAMA

for R.S.

Those times turning myself
into a tornado.
The man I saw
like a luminescent figure
in a flat landscape.
Or the man with hard edges,
stepping out of the misty crowd.
I'd watch him
and dream of being.

But now the soft focus is dissolved;
the landscape is so clear
I step into it,
and those tears dry up.
I tuck him under my arm
like a newspaper.
The line from my heart to his body
shrank
and I saw the map around it—
I saw the line become a road to somewhere.
I lose myself in the towns.

Still, sometimes, without a map,
I try the road alone,
and his image floats by,
dense as a storm that gathers along the horizon,
light as the flicker of the edge of a dream.

AMBIVALENCE

The rooms can breathe now that you've left.
The ocean, big O, fills the hall and my fuzzy head.
Tired of adjectives and nouns,
now I have a chance for verbs.
Now I have a chance to take walks.
The first layer of beige on your canvas
seeped through the rooms.
Now I'll remember myself, again.
Your angular self, tilting around the hall,
like a piece of paper—
what is it doing in big rooms on a new street?
Do you see how hard you are to talk to?
You're like a chip of granite
that, when I saw it,
made me feel warm.
I won't know what you're eating for dinner.
You won't know if I'm still hanging around.
I'll be listening to sounds more carefully.
This is like taking off a tight dress that I love.

SKYWRITING

I'm a thousand feet tall.
I use white chalk.
Each letter takes so long.
I'm sending you a message
that reads, "Listen to me!"
It's painful to write this large.

You're walking down Main Street.
Several people notice you. They say,
"Look up," but you're annoyed.
You're looking for the hardware store.
You're having a hard enough time finding it;
you can't be distracted like that.

Well, now I'm stooped over.
I'm sorry I ever did it.
Everyone saw my skywriting;
I forgot to put it in code.
After a while it smudged
and drifted away.

I have shrunk back to normal size.
An inch shorter, to tell the truth.
I'm walking down Main Street again
hoping I don't bump into you.

ELIZABETH

Elizabeth,
>born in a stadium
>by the pitcher's mound,
Elbowed
>through holders
>of autograph books,
Put on the glove,
>the gear,
>yelled,
Found she could play,
>played blacker
>than the rest.
Sit down.
>Now the crowd
>begins to gobble,
Chew Wrigleys.
>Soon they slap
>each other's faces.
Yanking each other
>by their collars
>off the bleachers,
They run to
>Elizabeth.
>She decrescendoes.
She pivots,
>leaving them
>breathless.
"I know,"
>she smiles savagely
>in bed
To her leaning husband
>who likes casseroles,
>"But not tonight."

CARMELLA

this isn't another letter, Carmella—
I know I haven't
kept in touch

you were rock-ribbed
pitiful a pile of purple bones rattle
who
sinewy, acute, in unknowable pain
cheekbones a foot long

I'm going to the movies tonight
you're rattling in the main room
of the ward, after twenty odd years.
Alyosha, what do you mean by happiness? who?
your sister every Christmas
dragged you to her grave
you killed our mother, you whore
you don't speak for years at a time, who?

Laura
came to see you months
after I heard you heard from Ruth
Who i uth? and you rattle on
that's a good sign, she recognized your name, who
playing cards for months
then silent except for occasional curses
can't do that ta me
who can't, Carmella?

they gave you black eyes
when you wouldn't shower

when you would shower
they laughed at your body who

it does no good
to remember you
I didn't understand
years later someone said
you were wrong to expect her
to care about you   who

on the way home from the hospital
three of us in the back seat of the station wagon
doing hear no evil see no evil speak no evil
Alyosha, what do you mean by happiness?
she knicked her wrist with Chiclet, chewed it,
blood and all, saying
that's what my breath smells like in the morning anyway

GIRL

Girl who slides below shadows,
who escapes into rooms at night,
and every morning has time to herself.

The girl with quiet clothes.

A line is broken in her mind.
She bends to collect wood
in the manmade forest.
She is listening intently
for someone to talk to.

Girl with broken shadows,
holding fragments.

Time moves around her like a wind.
There is storm in her voice.
There is no choice in her habits.

Thoughts like small fish
run out of her hands.

THE REST

Diamonds of the past
dazzle in the rear-view mirror.
The rest, dark pine trees,
I try to decipher.
Some punks in a father's car
smoke quickly
at the other end of the gravel lot.

Music moves because it compares:
silence to sound, short to long,
sweet to sour, dark to bright.
But I seem to have no senses,
just pieces of rope,
tugging in my head during the day
and into the night.

And so I drove to this field—
it's like ones where I used to dream
of perfect boys,
boys I could hold while they lectured
on freedom. Now
I dream of touching everyone more,
of getting mad when I want,
of my own soft eyes, hands, my heart.

MOSQUITO

Fine weather in the high country.
Good cups of coffee,
rich silence.
One of these days is broken
by a sentence from a woman
I usually like to see.
She hands me advice
that I don't want.
The sentence looms out
and hovers like a giant mosquito.
Whenever my reading lapses
the mosquito buzzes around me
until it settles on a piece of flesh
and nips away at me.
I call up the woman,
ask her to squash the mosquito for me.
This isn't so easy by this time,
but she comes over, attempts, succeeds.
She looks smooth now,
and I go back to drinking my coffee.

LOVE POEM

Outside it's pale blue.
Inside it's pale green.
There's a white muff
on the beige sofa of roses.
Let me smoothe your forehead.
Let my eyes soften.
Let me stop inquiring of everyone else
if I'm still alive.
I've been dulled for too long.
Let me show you
charcoal cats
wandering here,
gold bits of music,
the people of cinnamon and maroon.
Stay here.
Not as a woman would ask a man
I ask this, but as the moon
would ask the night.

CLAUDIA

claudia the cezanne in you the beige in you the could in you
claudia the crab you picked in the pebbles claudia
the sandpaper sounding its time in you claudia
your voice claudia in melted caramel
claudia encrusting the caramel claudia rust and solid
claudia the brown not desert landscape in you
claudia the thin hair too thin for your thickness claudia
claudia the hugging stirring you the fatigue halting you
claudia the c-l-a-u belong to you, the d your blue eyes
claudia the i is your hair too thin for your padded arms
maine is the name of the state for you you fit claudia
fit in the state like a chunk in arizona too
claudia the coral and salmon and beige in your dreams
claudia the people you pick they are black-haired and thin
        not claudia
claudia not like you claudia
claudia your voice half an octave lower than most
claudia the clouds pass over you laud you you click
claudia the ranch and the cattle and the rancher are you who
claudia own yourself and that's what you suit your taste to
claudia living is separate for you and you pick two to give to
and one always stays and one always leaves and claudia
claudia away I went still warmly and always to come back to you
claudia as you have painted me I want to paint you claudia

Barricades

BARRICADES

the task of beating down the barricades of habit and routine—
barricades which keep on rising.
—Benjamin Peret

Activity is not an illusion.
Comfort, but the readjustment of seasons.
Illusion is a primary activity.
We would hold onto one another if we could.

What hurts, what heals,
then what takes you away.
What you do with where you came from.
Are you asking the right questions.

Your eyes hurt, your hands are cold.
You are actively waiting.
The barricade is going to fall, again, soon.
For what. In back of the pleasing barricade

lies the warmth of pain, a barricade of
panic behind that, filtering the world.
And behind panic comes momentary peace.
The possibility of developing.

But the effort is always
difficult to the same degree.
You move away yet you turn toward it.
The tune this time is not yet audible,
not yet clear. The time, the tune,
the kind change with change, but the effort,
the effort always contains
the same degree of possibility.

THE PHILOSOPHER'S STONE

Mesmerized. I am earth, air, water.
Here, by a loud and sable fire
I find a blue and white snakeskin,
a rainbow dissolving,
lemon and sugar,
the edge of his lip.
O I see now, it's not
the fire I've wanted to be,
but the wood.
The fire is in its late fall.

the smell of burnt pyramids
      zebra stripes
the odor of burnt ozone
      fluid coils
the touch of burnt winds

To the left, white coral.
In the center, black velvet.
Crushed velvet and gold-sequined trim.
Brains and snails to the right.
In back, flies and Tyrannosaurus Rex.

The embers glow so deep.
At the end,
a slug looks on
from the sea of the fireplace.
Its eyes are not alive,
are white discs
that move
when people sleep.
The embers glow so
shrill, unnatural.

TWO WINDS

The day looks confused, like the swirling of a crowded brain.
The trees have no notion of why they were placed where they are,
and they have no one, not even each other, being separately placed.
A few flowers turn up their little noses, the snobs,
trying to catch a breath of air among the drunken weeds.
From the east and north two winds are blowing.
They hit each other in the face and fall down exhausted.
The rivers skirt the cities, they don't want to come closer,
but river rats swim through their bodies, small reminders.

The afternoon is surrounded, it can't break loose for hours.
People tug and grab at its center,
hoping to wrench out some happenings.
Some yellow and red boats are pleased with themselves,
but they've been fooled.
They are too garish for the landscape, which is
brown and maroon and a very pale blue.
The people can't decide whether to go out or wallow inside.
The fathers and mothers tear their hair today,
the children can't figure out which direction to go in.

The day knows that it will come around again, in a few months,
helpless as it is to stop itself.
The people now insist on stepping into it, and it cries
like the dried blood of a father who, after a battle,
returns to a family to whom he cannot talk.

SOME QUESTIONS AND ANSWERS

What is a manager?
A manager is someone who makes a statement.
What is a salesgirl?
A salesgirl is someone who asks a question.
What is a statement?
A statement is a principle of business.
What is a question?
Calm is the answer and the question.
What is anxiety?
The question and not the answer.
What is an oddity?
Someone who asks too many questions.
What is a cat, a lover, a TV?
The refusal to question and answer.
Have you anything to add?
A long line to add, like a rope pulling you through a cave.
What is a cave?
A cave is a place where you are not free, and want to be.
What is a home?
A home is a cave filled with questions and answers.

WHEN YOU CALL ME

When you call me I come,
mother, husband, boss, professor.
I can yell back,
but I always care.
Other times, other people
fade in your sunlight,
shrink in your darkness.
I am other people and I hole up
in some shadow,
in the ink that stays
in the jar.
I am afraid to go in the car:
who knows what might happen
traveling in another person's world.

RED DREAM

Small hills on fire,
orange, red.
A desert,
five little buildings.
Gas station shaped like a pump.
You parked the car,
and I walked into the church
to wait for you.
But the car wouldn't go up the ramp.
You had to drive around again.
In this way I lost you.
Men robbing the church
noticed me standing in the hall.
I smiled,
pretending I had seen nothing,
so they left me alone.
I went out to the parking lot.
A woman
with a little white dog
was asking for directions.

ICE AND WATER

Young girl with icicles
all around her house.
The sun's reflections in the ice
scare her.
Tall men arrive
to sell her things.
Thin men,
with vests.
She's tired as history
but can't sleep.
Behind her house
salmon jump upstream
to spawn in the curative waters,
miraculous to her, though she is so young.

EGG CARTONS, RADIATORS, TENTS

There was nothing precious; I was moving.
And all these things were unresolved.

There was no poem coming, coercing
gell. After emotional conversation
I found myself alone.

And all these things beside me
are things all unresolved.

I swear (I whisper)
all these things beside me
are my stream, a gush,
are my stone.

(Good morning.)
There was no answer.
I stopped
looking, my life was calm.

(All these things beside me
and all things unresolved.)

Tentacles are all we have,
myopic, drawn.
But when old ones are ripped, new ones bloom.

CONSTRAINT

Like the clouds I'm stuck in the middle,
emotions above and below.
I could be married in the morning,
but night is a hill of molecules.
Constraint, I've lived with you,
I can't condemn you, because I chose you.
Your traces cover my body.
You're in the insides of my thighs,
on my stomach, in my cheekbones, my smile.
I breathe and breath is wasted,
forced into pockets and corners,
refused extension.
The long, still heartbreak,
which annoys us in others,
cuts the current from the brain to the heart,
from the heart to the body,
from the body to love.

THE DAY

is a constant,
                that which arches around itself,

                        a window partly covered
                        in varying degrees
                        by the shade;

            is a summary,
              separated by two shadows;
            is a blink;
                the days are a series.

The day is visual,
            all day.
The day is tactile,
            with luck.
The day is oral,
            in patches.
The day is almost always
                in two dimensions.

And this has not been easy for us—
the day is a time when we are not breathing.

We bounce off each other like rubber,
our mouths move like rubber,
the violins make us melancholy.

            The mail, the furniture,
                the cooking
        keep us.

In general the body has this way of
            connecting:
that two eyes exist and pull everything
            through.

This is confusion, this.
This is rigidity.
This is a line in the head,
a calendar in the body.
This is a map of the world we are living with.

            The day
                        is a curve of two dimensions that arches
            back on itself and forgets to breathe.
            There is always the past in this sense.
            The day is a movement of bushes in the desert.

The arch could be a rainbow,
but the day has washed-out colors,
or else the day comes pulsing,
too rich and then too long.

We have days like chamelions running across the road.

The days are bridled.
The man is dry.
He goes to the tide.
He has days of wanting
                        to shut everything down
                                                and go home.
The time is invisible.
The days are filled with space like the shell of a body.

The day
        goes down like a cliff.
                        It is attached to us.
                                It is impossible
for most of us to go over it.

                        The day
        is a constant, is a skin,
        and we are drums,
                        and the world is blinking now,
                                and the tide

is an arch that curves over itself.

Landscapes

JERUSALEM

Black summers have baked the yellow stone.
Now wall and earth inseparable: a thickly floored hole.
Fat dress-and-scarf-drenched woman.
Under a grey stone a lizard squints.
Past here are watches,
but now, in the simmer of a weekly afternoon,
a small drum, answering the shofar, here, where
women dumped their babies on the pointed rock.

From inside the earth I feast on
feet of the one-eyed Arab.
A Chosid gently touches, presses my stone, drinks
warm water, comes again.
A soldier builds orange fire. It can't burn me more.
More than a few men have died or run away from
the stinging of eyes pierced by stone.

Thin, loud-mouthed brown children display
pens, dough, clothespins, beads,
badger among the tinkle of copper for half a lira.
All have half an eye, then two:
one for the flies, the other for money.
Chickens peck at cucumbers; in the market
old pictures of Lauren Bacall, glass ducks,
keychains, glass, Bebsi, glass, orange drink.

Inside, felafel and more flies.
Everyone smokes.
Girls walk holding hands, push.
A dry mouth behind a black veil spits at me.

A SHADOW

". . . To me
It speaks of a lot of other things,
Memories and longings
And things that never were."

"You never heard the wind pass by
The wind speaks of the wind only.
What you heard from it was a lie,
And the lie's in you."
——Fernando Pessoa

Today January was so warm
we lay side by side without touching,
drifting on pine needles,
surrounded by melting snow.

Neither looked at the other,
but at the sky, at the trees' weavings.
We heard snow drip noisily from branches,
smelled the clarity of weather.

I would always lie under the pine trees.

I heard your body turn towards mine.
Unconsciously mine moved towards yours—
I saw your eyes, what I wanted to avoid—

I saw my mind as a city dying,
and something else was being born:
I was afraid I'd given birth to a shadow.

I thought the trees told me that.
The trees told me nothing, my thoughts
were melancholy lies
suspending freedom.

Tonight I've returned to my city
and all the things you said you left.
I begin to understand another thing:
that my mind has to hear the sounds of snow.

IN THE GARDEN

Words were written large in her family:
April, woman, garden.
A black bird slid down the wind
like the palm of her hand.
Along the path,
the cherry blossoms fogged.
The spiked tiger lilies
didn't pierce her eyes.
But a scent unraveled her,
at a bush of yellow roses—
she was suddenly too happy.
The happiness of dusk, she called it.
The leaving of colors, fading of scents.
Knowing this, she stopped walking.

THE STEPS OF MONTMARTRE

From the top steps—
Paris at seven,
lavender at dusk.

Pigeons landed on boys' fists
to nibble seed. Only two boys,
arms out, would do.

Folding chairs
carried step to step
to see the new.

Old men,
left half way up,
breathed heavily.

The very chic
were not there.
The city,

covered by sunset,
dissolved into stars.
Bells, a whisper.

Cathedral.
Purple sky,
white lights.

ON THE BOAT

Sometimes I feel like a Rorschach test.
The world sees what it wants in me
and I become its bat's wings,
its butterfly, its map of a body.

Still, on an island
of silence and sun
I don't get lonely.
On an island I don't
mind being by myself.

But on the boat,
gliding back to the city,
my mind gets choppy.
I want to eat.
I want to talk.

I say to myself,
"You have a
long boatride ahead of you."

But there are no controls.
The world is looking at me.
It sees a woman going somewhere,
back to where the people are.

NEW ORLEANS

Lope de Vega.
Yellow.
O. That.
You. And a sun.
Early. Green.
Hat. Green.
O swim cold blue.
Cockatoo.
O good. Walk.
Vacancy.
Look and look
and look and look.
White.
White.
Palm. Surprise.
Sand sounds.
Word hard.
Walk a sun.
Courtyard.
Still. A
Try. A
Week. A
black happiness.

A DESCRIPTION

Orange popsicles.
And the women and men are swimming.
As long as there's a sun.
As long as the sun is strong.
As a long thing the sun is.
The towels are flat and rippled.
Bodies are heated up.
The skin is changing.
The sand.
The trashcans are red.
Everywhere I turn is sun.
The men and women are clean.
The ocean is salt.
Ocean translucent and olive.
Not watching the men and women.
The worshippers of the sun.
As long as the sun is shining.
The sand is clean.
Is moving.
As long as the sun.
As long as the shadows.
A sand.
An afterglow of sun.

THE BOOK, THE CITY

A black pool of gutter rain curves into a comma.
Cars spurt like dashes, trees cut like slashes,
street lights tint the ladies like quotation marks.
Semicolon; edge of the sidewalk.

In the morning, people weave through the streets like sentences.
Two people bump each other: a parenthetical remark.
Lines of people wait for buses in clauses.
Powerful capital letters push to the fronts of the lines.
That woman is a noun; her clothes, layers of adjectives.
Someone is seen running in italics. *A foreigner.*

When three happy people stroll together
they comprise a simple sentence.
When they caress one another
their writing turns from printing into script.

At mid-afternoon, houses square off like brackets.
Scattered bushes glisten like asterisks.
Climbing some stairs, we skim a long quotation.
Each pet yelps like an accent mark.

The city is a book; the sun the title.
And rivers move with little noise, like spaces.
A period ends the day.
Last words dissolve into dreams,
the newspapers into Oriental rugs.

When in dreams bombs demolish the city
grammar breaks down completely.
Exclamation marks flutter.
Only the moon stays clear.

MEADOW IN MAINE

My profile in the rear-view mirror:
yellow and red dots of color.
When I come back
I'll be hard again,
like schedules and formica.

Off the highway
mosquitoes graze,
rust-colored bushes twinkle,
pines stand around like mothers,
moths like white flowers flick.

I'm not as pretty as I was.
My friend's reading in the car.
Short time to daydream
what I imagine I was.

COLLAGE

In a corner of Boston—
a group of buildings,
above another group of buildings,
across the street,
in the distance,
pastel green and blue.
Under the full moon,
they reminded me of San Francisco,
which reminded me of you.

Maybe they still are
and do.

I looked around.
No one was watching.
There was the trolley.
I put the moon in a box
and got on it.

OCEAN

Old people come here
to not move anymore,
smell like the sea.
Some tiny snail frying.
A teardrop,
lost in winds of waves:
the unfastening of a thought
from the body.

TOY BOAT

toy boat
toy boat
toy boat
toy boat
That
which we know
we find
most difficult
to pronounce:

A machine gun
chops impressively,
the quiet wars of China
continue:

bodies
        float downstream
                discover
            their brothers

See the stare of the present
in the eyes
of these
white ducks
watching the toy boat watching

HOURS

Five matches to light my cigarette.
I'm surprised I can notice a bush with
    extraordinary purple flowers
    between me and the river.
When I've left you may
    notice this bush, or ones like it.
When I come back,
Some things about you will surpise me.
Of course there are purple flowers there, too—
    extraordinary. Really.
A Japanese woman with purple shorts
    has appeared out of nowhere,
    stands on the rock
    in back of the bush,
And I am gone to the new place already,
    although just hours ago I was
    still here,
    shimmering in the hot day,
    cooling myself by the river.

Hieroglyphs

BEAR

The only beautiful dream left to me from childhood:
My limbs cascading over the white picket fence
to the bright mansion next door,
where I ran with baby bears through gorgeous rooms.
We gorged ourselves on honey
from large cream-colored earthenware jars.
Light ran in, like paler honey, from tall windows there.

I'm a stubborn woman:
I fear a thousand nameless, bodiless things,
and still refuse to wake myself
when the tracks of a bear surround my camp.

FIELDS

Often I am permitted to return to a meadow
                                    —Robert Duncan

There's the meadow of the bed.
When there's a timelessness about it, it's real;
when there's not, not.

There's the field of dreams,
which only seems to have time.
Which is.

There's the field of the poem.
When all my other meadows are,
I'm permitted to enter.

Of course there's no time.
Then the poem
moves through the others,
defining its own limits.

The fields criss-cross, mingle.

Occasionally the meadow of the poem
enters the meadow of the dream.
Letters twenty feet tall
stand on the mountain, calling me.
I climb them.
I am the letter E, red and black.
I fall forward, pedalling a bicycle all over the hills.

LAST NIGHT I DREAMED THE REVOLUTION

This morning I got up early,
felt proud and easy.
Until, hours later, a fog
over the sand, I go walking,
ripples cascading under my feet.
I want to walk softly.
A dog barks, I don't need to pet him.
I touch the waves
and my feet push down the melting sand.
I hear things one at a time.
I touch my arm,
my hand is incredibly gentle.

If snow were streaming through the air
it would make the world
no more silent.

POSSESSIONS

In the springtime
one becomes
overwhelmed by possessions
and the impulse
to throw the clothes away,
the books away,
the house away,
the body away.
Anxiety,
the inability
to do this.
I continue
to stare at
the objects,
overcome
by the desire
to clean them up
at least.
A wish finally not
to clean up the old body
but to find a new one.
Or at least
clean the rug.
Or at least
throw the rug away
and polish the floor.
Or at least
scrape the polish
off the floor.
Scrub it beige,
run your fingers over it.

Or at least
not touch it at all,
just stare.
Or at least
let it be there
but never glance at it.
Or at least
say it never existed.

FISH IN E FLAT

pearl leeri
stay away from me

your friend
bubble eyes
tries to break the glass
with his stare

lyretail molly glides
Greek Appalachian
in a goldfish bowl

head tail lite
don' feel nothin'
but you light up the night

tinfoil barb
starts a silver war
so blood fin
can slice through the mane

wood cat
jes plain
saw that

banjo catfish
living down South
catching a musical mouse

brown ghost
heads a Thanksgiving parade

imperial sword crinkel
tinkles

SCIENCE FICTION DREAM

South Texas was a large breast.
Three men lived their lives on its plains, on its hills.
And the sky—it loomed with dusty particles of clouds.
Through the layers of clouds three U.F.O.'s,
 shining and round, three silvery discs, drifted down.
But they exploded like small atomic bombs,
killing all vegetation.
The three men walked some distance apart
through the stubble, sand, and weeds,
yellowish, frayed, and brittle.
Did these men know each other?
It seemed that they did, but then they hid from one another.
The first one was wild,
and screamed at the second from behind a dead bush.
The third scared himself and tried to huddle alone.
All three went back to their apartments eventually,
all on Main Street, on the first floor.
The second one was about to close his door and pack,
when the first one yelled,
"Stay where you are, you have no right to move."
I am the second man now, become a woman,
a woman who is about to take the last bus out of south Texas.
For the first time, the breast, the atomic bomb,
the man yelling, the man hiding can't reach me.
I can stay calm, get on the bus,
and walk into my present.
At the end of this dream, I can see
something I had stopped believing
I could catch in time—
a bus leaving now for my real home.

HARD WORK

When the night is dry and the air is old
I remember that I have really forgotten.
I leave the table,
come inside to my room,
and ask for hard work.
I ask many times,
and at first the way is remote,
until it melts,
until the melody is clear,
until the colors deepen.
The music and asteroids enter,
while old loves move inside me.
My mind curves into the sky,
turns like a great whale,
plays like an organ,
whispers,
cries as if I had just seen
my first lover.

If I can listen long enough
to the melodies that early peoples and spiders made,
decorating the earth—
my smile will stay genuine,
my face will be genuine.

VISITING

I have come to this space through many rooms.
Here, there is no telling.
Your words frightened me;
here, your sound won't carry.
This looks like a circle,
where the days can't pass, but turn.
I have no robes—
unlike a monk, I am visiting.
Under all my complaints lay a loneliness.
Now, I chose to come here, alone,
to think of you,
to try to love you.
Take your care, hand it back to yourself,
turn to your room and rest there—
Today I have one space that is all light
and no decoration.
Time was a longing. Let go,
go into the light.

SOUND WITHOUT TONE

So long the tow of the tide pulled me down.
The water force-fed me, I was spitting it out.
I flung myself down on the wet sand.
It took too long to find the tall grasses.
And now, they're only single steps away.
They breathe so quietly.
My feet press into the mud; I'm grounded.
Further along, the earth is dry, and cool.
I lie down, brush my cheek along the yielding grasses.
I have no mouth. I have strong hands.
There is no you, for a moment.
Lying in the mild grass, I remember the ocean.
The ocean becomes a memory so quickly.
How surprising that I should welcome night, and quiet.
I want to stay in a place that is all mine,
and not at all mine.
A place all new,
where the jewels of the sun
and the molecules of the night
are one. And love,
like a sound without tone,
drifting along the whispering grasses.

HIEROGLYPHS

Words of dreams I can almost remember.
Brushstroke, clue to seeing.
Walking in clear air.

Little owls and blackbirds,
people who look like fingers,
lines of lightning, rods
of power, and the mysterious
circle with a dot sitting on three legs.
Mystery, but in a playful mood.
Storks and beetles,
fish and half-circles,
patiently waiting for another century.

Love as a series of angles,
hieroglyphs you've hidden, love.
An ache when I can't see them.
When suddenly I can read them, what peace.